MORE 303 FIDDLE TUNES

Compiled by

RON MIDDLEBROOK

PUBLISHER EXTRODINAIRE

ISBN: 978-1-57424-244-7
SAN 683-8022

Book cover design by James Creative Group

Layout by Kenny Warfield

Copyright © 2009 CENTERSTREAM Publishing, LLC
P.O. Box 17878 - Anaheim Hills, CA 92817

www.centerstream-usa.com

Table Of Contents

Reels

Jigs

Hornpipes

Clogs

Strathspeys

Harold Crosby, Charles Ross Taggatt and Dan Ross.

THE JIG

The Jig tends toward running eights in 6/8 time, with the accents falling on beats one and four (ONE two three FOUR five six). Sixteenths are counted by saying "and" after the beat containing the sixteenth note, and usually occur in the pickup measure of the tune. Jigs are not to be played fast.

"Irish Washerwoman"

THE REEL

The reel usually tends towards running, or continuous eighths (with occasional quarter notes), in common time. Eighth notes in four-four time are counted by saying "and" after each beat. Here are some common rhythms:

Subdividing the beat into three produces triplets, counted as "**ONE triplet TWO triplet**,"etc. Here are some examples:

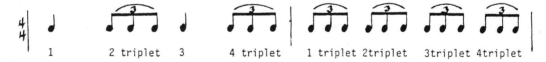

Reels, particulary Irish reels, often combine eighth notes and triplets (The Wise Maid, Swallowtail Reel, and Mason's Apron are all examples). Here's what they look like together:

Sometimes reels can be played with a "backbeat", that is, placing the accent on the second and fourth beats rather than on the usual first and third beats. A backbeat will provide more of a southern-type feel to the tune. Certain Irish fiddlers, such as Kevin Burke for one, play with a strong backbeat. You can experiment with the reels and see for yourself which of them sound good this way. **The reel is the fastest type of dance tune.**

THE HORNPIPE

There seems to be a certain amount of confusion surrounding hornpipes, as they are almost never played the way they are written. For the sake of convience, hornpipes are written in dotted four-four with triplet ornamentation, but in practice they are played in 12/8 time. The rhythm figure of dotted eighth-sixteenth ♪ is intended to be played as a quarter-eighth triplet (also known as "swing" eighths). This would be written as ♪ ♪ or ♪♪ (a curved line connecting two notes of the same pitch is called a tie, and joins the time values of the two notes).

Here are some common hornpipe rhythms.

The confusion that sometimes surrounds hornpipes also stems from the fact that many hornpipes are played without accentation, and thus come closer to being treated as reels than as hornpipes. This accounts for the inclusion of "Staten Island Hornpipe" with the reels. "Fisher's Hornpipe" is also commonly played as a reel in this country, but I prefer it as a hornpipe. Hornpipes are generally played more slowly than reels, and can also be played with a backbeat.

—————————— Metronome setting are generally: ——————————
Double Jig 127- ♪.
Single Jig 137- ♪.
Slip Jig 144- ♪.
Reel 224- ♪
Hornpipe 180- ♪

○

THE WALTZ

Waltzes are played in three-four time with the beat subdivided into eighths or triplets. The strong beat falls on the count of "one" (ONE, two, three, ONE, two, three, etc.)

Here are some examples of common waltz rhythms:

Waltzes should be played with a gentle, swaying feel.

Country dances usually end with a waltz.

SET DANCES AND MISCELLANEOUS

Set Dances are simply tunes to which different specific dances have been set.

Old Time Music Contests

Ken Perlman

Instrument-competitions have had a major role in the development of old-time music in the twentieth century. In order to more fully understand the music we play, it makes sense to take a look at how these contests originated and developed.

Much has been made in the literature of fiddle contest held as part of a St Andrews Day celebration in the Williamsburg, Virginia area in 1736, which offered a "fine Cremona fiddle" as first prize. Given the time frame, however, it can be inferred that the music played at this event would almost certainly have borne small resemblance to what we now think of as fiddling. For one thing, the kind of music we now call "reels" (the parent-genre of Southern breakdowns) was just coming into its own in the Highlands of Scotland, and was then virtually unknown outside its home area. More important, the date precedes by about a decade the emergence of Niel Gow, the Scottish musician who is generally credited with developing the powerful rhythmically-articulated sawstroke technique that ultimately served as the foundation for fiddling.

Throughout the nineteenth century, fiddlers' conventions were frequently held in the towns and villages of the United States, often on the courthouse lawn in conjunction with the arrival of the local circuit court. Although the term "fiddlers' convention" is associated with contests nowadays, it is not at all clear that competition was a major aspect of these nineteenth century gatherings. Instead, these "conventions" seem for the most part to have been just what the name implies: occasions for conviviality, swapping tunes and telling stories. Concerts featuring fiddle playing would often be held in association with these events, with proceeds going to support local schools or other public causes.

Competitions involving only fiddling begin to come into play in certain parts of the US beginning about the last third of the nineteenth century (banjos and other fretted instruments don't really come into the old-time contest picture until much later). There are records of fiddle contests taking place in Atlanta, Georgia as early as the 1870s. In the 1880s and 90s, fiddle contests were held alongside citywide holiday festivities in Knoxville, Tennessee. A thriving fiddle contest scene grew up in west Texas near Amarillo around the turn of the twentieth century. In 1907, an eight-day contest—eventually won by future Grand Ol' Opry star Uncle Jimmy Thompson—was held in Dallas. In 1913, an annual contest was established in Atlanta and continued there for over twenty years.

Some of these early contest scenes were the breeding grounds for many of the first successful commercial old-time music entertainers. I have already mentioned Uncle Jimmy Thompson. Eck Robertson—the first southern fiddler to record on a major label—was a product of the West Texas contest scene. Fiddlin' John Carson—probably the first southern fiddler to play on radio, and the first country-music artist to produce a commercially successful recording, came out of the Atlanta contest scene. Other products of Atlanta contests include such well-known artists as Gid Tanner, Clayton McMichen and Lowe Stokes, all three of whom played with the famous Skillet Lickers Band.

It is interesting to note that in most cases, contests were established in particular areas only after local community fiddle-dance scenes had begun to decline. This interpretation seems born out by the comments of organizers or observers. For example, William Van Jacoway, who organized a contest in De Kalb Country, Alabama hoped by way of this event "to perpetuate the memory and the music of the old-time fiddle, to revere the past, [and] to show the present generation…. that there was sweeter and more inspiring music emanating from the fiddle and the bow than will ever be found in the present day jazz." (From the De Kalb Republican, Aug. 14, 1924).

The true heyday of these contests in terms of media interest came in the mid-1920s as a result of famed industrialist Henry Ford's campaign to revive fiddling and square dancing throughout the United States. Ford's campaign—which ad its roots in an avowed aim to rid American music and dance of its foreign and Afro-American influences—got underway in 1923 when he began holding old-time dances at an inn he purchased in Sudbury, Massachusetts. In 1925, he sponsored a contest in Detroit at which 80-year old Jasper "Jep" Bisbee of Michigan was crowned "King of Old-time Fiddlers." Not long afterwards, a fiddler of similar vintage named Mellie Dunham of Norway, Maine received national publicity when Ford invited him to spend a few days as his personal guest in Dearborn, Michigan (there was talk at the time of setting up a grudge-match with North vs. South overtones between Uncle Jimmy Thompson and Dunham, but it never came off).

By 1926 media interest in fiddling was at an all time high, and literally hundreds of contests were held that year all over North America. In January 26, for example, the three-day "All New England Contest" was held in Providence, Rhode Island, involving dozens of contestants and thousands of spectators. In April, the four-day "World Champion Old-Time Fiddlers' Contest" was held in Lewiston, Maine. Included among its contestants was none other than well-known Scottish fiddle great James Scott Skinner. The biggest contest of all was national in scope: some 1,865 fiddlers competed in local and regional playoffs organized through Ford dealerships. In a "playoff" held in Detroit, Uncle Bunt Stephens of Lewisburg, Tennessee was declared national champion.

Although national interest in old-time music competitions paled after 1927 and plummeted at the onset of the Great Depression, contests at the local and regional levels continued to be held in many areas through the 1930s. In the mid 30s, a promoter named Larry Sunbrock created a touring, commercialized version of the fiddle contest in which well known players such as Fiddlin' Arthur Smith and Clayton McMichen would face-off with lesser lights. As in modern professional wrestling. The outcomes of these matches were often predetermined. Few old-time contests of any kind were held through the 1940s, although the now famous Union Grove Fiddlers' Convention (which has run continuously since its foundling in 1924) was a notable exception.

Most of the larger old-time fiddling contests around nowadays have grown up with the fiddle association movement, which started in the early 1950s. About 1950, the Canadian Open Old-Time Fiddlers' Contest was founded in Shelburne, Ontario. In 1953, a small, annual fiddle contest was established at Weiser, Idaho by amateur folklorist Blaine Stubblefield. In 1962 the event was taken over by the newly formed Idaho Old-Time Fiddlers' Association, and renamed The National Old-Time Fiddlers' Contest (interestingly, the 1973 Senior Division prize at "The National" was won by none other than Eck Robertson!). Before long, comparable groups had formed in Missouri (1962), Montana ('63), Oregon ('64), Nebraska ('64) and Vermont ('65). By the mid-seventies, fiddle associations had also formed in Washington, California, Kansas, Illinois, Tennessee, Indiana, Texas, and Wyoming and British Columbia.

For most of these organizations, sponsoring contests ultimately became the most important activity. Essentially, organizers simply felt that offering members the opportunity to compete was the best way to maintain their interest in playing.

How have contests affected the practice of old-time music? For one thing, as contests replace playing-for-dances as the major focus of old-time music, there is a strong tendency for musicians to de-emphasize strong dance rhythms in favor of the kind of smooth, showy virtuosity that impresses judges. This was certainly one of the factors that led to the rise in the mid-to-late 1920s of the "long-bow" style (many notes off a single stroke), which now dominates bluegrass, swing and contest fiddling nationwide. Another common theme—also noted by those who have studied the effects of Scottish and Irish traditional music competitions—is that contests tend to quickly push up the general level of expertise, but they also tend to create homogenization among players. In other words, because those eager to succeed soon adopt the general approach of previous contest winners, both individual idiosyncrasies and variation among regional styles tend to be suppressed.

[Main sources: Mary Anne Alburger: "Scottish Fiddlers and Their Music"; Richard Blaustein: "Traditional Music and Social Change" (thesis); Joyce Cauthen: "With Fiddle and Well-Rosined Bow: Old-Time Fiddling in Alabama"; Steve Greene: "Uncle Joe Shippee and the All New England Fiddle Contest" (pamphlet); Earl Spielman: "Traditional North American Fiddling" (thesis); Charles R. Townsend: "San Antonio Rose: The Life and Music of Bob Wills"; Gene Wiggins, "Fiddlin' Georgia Crazy: Fiddlin' John Carson, His Real World…"; Charles Wolfe, The Devil's Box: Masters of Southern Fiddling"; Charles Wolfe, "Tennessee Strings"]

Charles Ross Taggatt

reels

The Reel is a ring dance, often called a round dance. Originally this dance had Pagan religious meanings and was thought to be evil by the early Christian Church. The reel continues to be the most popular form with Scots Traditional players. The Scots play the reel a little slower then the Irish, and the tunes are more chordal in structure, whereas the Irish play their reels quite fast.

Metronome setting 224- ♩

Abitha Muggins' Favorite Reel
All The Way to Galway Reel
Ally Croaker's Favorite Reel
Arbana Reel
Bennett's Favorite Reel
Blackberry Blossom Reel
Blackwater Reel
The Bonnie Lad Reel
The Boyne Hunt Reel
Brooklyn Lasses Reel
Buckley's Favorite Reel
Cameronian Reel
Cape Cod Reel
Captain Kelley's Reel
Charming Katy's Reel
Congress Park Reel
Connaught Lasses Reel
Connemara's Pet reel
Corkonian Reel
Corporal Casey's Fancy Reel
The Countess Of Louden's Reel
The Cup Of Tea Reel
Daffy, Don't You Reel
Diamond Reel
Eyes Right Reel
Fill Up The Bowl Reel
Fire Fly Reel
Five Leaved Clover Reel
Flogging Reel
Flowers Of Cahirciveen Reel
Flowers Of Edinburg

Foxie Mary Reel
From Night Till Morn Reel
Green Grow The Rushes Reel
Green Hills Of Tyrol Reel
Hit Or Miss Reel
Hobb's Favorite Reel
Honeymoon Reel
Over Young To Marry Yet Reel
Inman Line Reel
Irish-American Reel
Jenny's Baby Reel
Johnny's Gone to France Reel
The Jolly Clam Digger's Reel
The Jolly Tinker's Reel
Judy's Reel
Judy Maley's Reel
Kiss Me, Joe Reel
Kiss The Bride Reel
Kitty Clover's Reel
Lady Edmonton's Reel
Lady Forbe's Reel
Lady Gardner's Reel
Lardner's Reel
Last Night's Fun Reel
The Lavender Girl Reel
Laven's Favorite Reel
League And Slasher Reel
Leap Year Reel
Levantine's Barrel Reel
Liverpool Jack's Reel
Lord Dalhousie's Reel

Lord Gordon's Reel
Maggie Picking Cockels Reel
Maid Of Athens Reel
The Masons' Cap Reel
May Pole Reel
The Miller's Maid Reel
Mill-Town Maid Reel
Miss Brown's Reel
Miss Corbett's Reel
Miss McDonald's Reel
Molly McGuire's Reel
Morton's Reel
My Love Is Far Away Reel
Ned Kendall's Favorite Reel
Niel Gow's Reel
Old Maids Of Galway Reel
Parnell's Reel
Queen's Guard Reel
The Rakish Highlander Reel
Rising Sun Reel
Rose Of The Valley Reel
Saratoga Reel
Ships Are Sailing Reel
Teetotaler's Reel
Three Merry Sisters Reel
Whiddon's Favorite Reel
Wide Awake Reel
You Bet Reel

Abitha Muggins' Favorite Reel

All The Way to Galway Reel

Ally Croaker's Favorite Reel

Arbana Reel

Bennett's Favorite Reel

Blackberry Blossom Reel

Blackwater Reel

The Bonnie Lad Reel

The Boyne Hunt Reel

Brooklyn Lasses Reel

Buckley's Favorite Reel

Cameronian Reel

Cape Cod Reel

Captain Kelley's Reel

Charming Katy's Reel

Congress Park Reel

Connaught Lasses Reel

Connemara's Pet Reel

Corkonian Reel

Corporal Casey's Fancy Reel

The Countess Of Louden's Reel

The Cup Of Tea Reel

Daffy, Don't You Reel

Diamond Reel

Eyes Right Reel

Fill Up The Bowl Reel

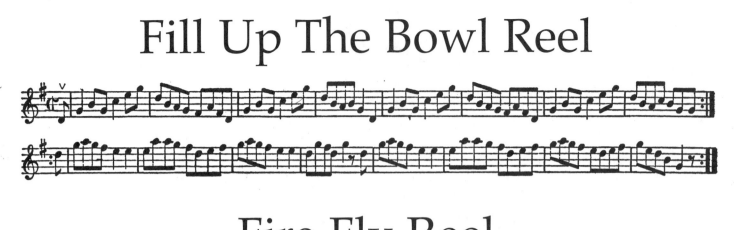

Fire Fly Reel

Five Leaved Clover Reel

Flogging Reel

Flowers Of Cahirciveen Reel

Flowers Of Edinburg

Foxie Mary Reel

From Night Till Morn Reel

Green Grow The Rushes Reel

Green Hills Of Tyrol Reel

Hit Or Miss Reel

Hobb's Favorite Reel

Honeymoon Reel

I'm Over Young To Marry Yet Reel

Inman Line Reel

Irish-American Reel

Jenny's Baby Reel

Johnny's Gone to France Reel

The Jolly Clam Digger's Reel

The Jolly Tinker's Reel

Judy's Reel

Judy Maley's Reel

Kiss Me, Joe Reel

Kiss The Bride Reel

Kitty Clover's Reel

Lady Edmonton's Reel

Lady Forbe's Reel

Lady Gardner's Reel

Lardner's Reel

Last Night's Fun Reel

The Lavender Girl Reel

Laven's Favorite Reel

League And Slasher Reel

Leap Year Reel

Levantine's Barrel Reel

Liverpool Jack's Reel

Lord Dalhousie's Reel

Lord Gordon's Reel

Maggie Picking Cockels Reel

Maid Of Athens Reel

The Masons' Cap Reel

May Pole Reel

The Miller's Maid Reel

Mill-Town Maid Reel

Miss Brown's Reel

Miss Corbett's Reel

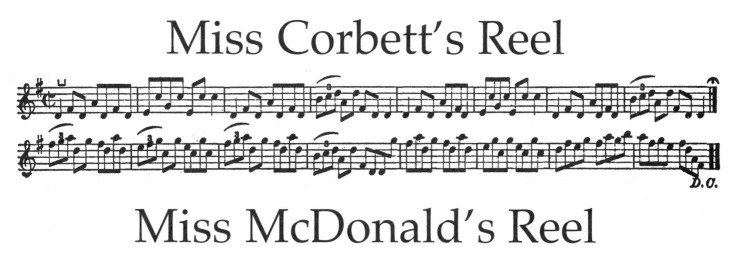

Miss McDonald's Reel

Molly McGuire's Reel

Morton's Reel

My Love Is Far Away Reel

Ned Kendall's Favorite Reel

Niel Gow's Reel

Old Maids Of Galway Reel

Parnell's Reel

Queen's Guard Reel

The Rakish Highlander Reel

Rising Sun Reel

Rose Of The Valley Reel

Saratoga Reel

Ships Are Sailing Reel

Teetotaler's Reel

Three Merry Sisters Reel

Whiddon's Favorite Reel

Wide Awake Reel

You Bet Reel

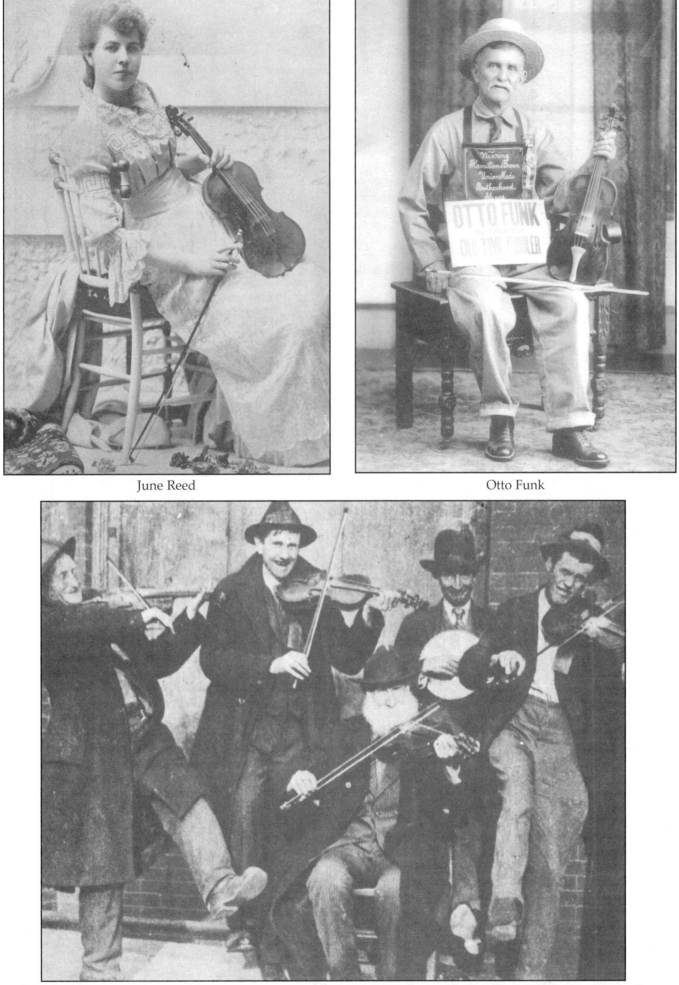

June Reed

Otto Funk

(l to r) Unidentified, Fiddlin' John Carson, Land Norris-Banjo Earl Johnson, Unidentified, Unidentified (seated)

JÍGS

Jigs are very popular dance tunes. In the 16th century, the word "Jigg" could be applied to any light tune, a joke, or a poor man's entertainment that had occasional dancing in one of the cheaper playhouses of the day.

Shakespeare immortalized the word when he used the expression to "Jigg off a tune" from the *Love's Labour's Lost* play. According to Alistair Anderson, the Slip Jig is a particutarly beautiful dance once the trick of never allowing the feet to touch the ground has been mastered.

Metronome Setting:
Double Jig 127- ♪· Single Jig 137- ♪· Slip Jig 144- ♪·

Bully For You Jig
Bundle And Go Jig
Butcher's March Jig
Butter Milk Mary's Jig
Buttermilk And Prattees Jig
Castle Garden Jig
Cat In The Hopper Jig
Catch Club Jig
Close To The Floor Jig
Come To The Raffle Jig
Come Under My Dimity
Connaught Man's Ramble Jig
Cowboy's Jig
Drink Of Brandy Jig
Drunken Gauger's Jig
Dublin Boy's Jig
Dusty Bob's Jig
Dusty Miller's Jig
Emon Acnuck Jig
Farewell, Sweet Nora Jig
Fasten The Wig On Her Jig
Flaming O'Flanigan's Jig
Fox Hunter's Jig
Frogs' Frolic Jig
The Gobby O' Jig
Golliber's Frolic Jig
Hare In The Corn Jig
Harrington's Hall Jig
Haste To The Wedding Jig
Hills Of Glenurchie Jig

Hop Jig
Humors Of Castle Lion Jig
Humour Of Glen Jig
Hunt The Fox Jig
Irish American Jig
Jackson's Rolling Jig
Johnny Hand's Jig
The Joy's Of Wedlock Jig
Katy Is Waiting Jig
Lady Cawdor's Jig
Lafrican's Jig
Lanigan's Ball Jig
Light And Airy Jig
Little Brown Jug Jig
The Limerick Lass Jig
Love Link's Jig
The Maid's Complaint Jig
Maloney's Fancy Jig
The Market Girl's Jig
Moll Roe In The Morning Jig
Moll Roe's Jig
Mount Your Baggage Jig
Mrs. Hogan's Goose Jig
The Munster Lass Jig
My Pretty, Fair Maid Jig
Mysteries Of Knock Jig
Neapolitan Threshers' Jig
The Night Of The Fun Jig
Night Of The Fair Jig
Old Figary O' Jig
Old Mother Goose Jig

Old Walls Of Liscarroll Jig
Over Land And Sea Jig
Owny's Best Jig
The Oyster Girl's Jig
Paddy O'Carrol's Jig
Paddy's The Boy Jig
Paddy's Farewell To America Jig
Pandeen O'Rafferty Jig
Parnell And Ireland Jig
Pat In His Glory Jig
The Pausteen Fawn Jig
The Pivot Brig Jig
Prince Charles' Jig
Puss In The Corner Jig
The Rakes Of Westmeath' Jig
Ride A Mile Jig
Roaring Willies' Jig
Rocky Road To Dublin Jig
Rough Diamond Jig
Sam Hide's Jig
Skin The Pealer Jig
The Soldier's Cloak Jig
Spirits Of Whiskey Jig
Strop The Razor Jig
Sunday Is My Wedding Day Jig
To Cashell I'm Going Jig
Trip To Galway Jig
Two Penny Postman's Jig
Vaughan's Favorite Jig

Bully For You Jig

Bundle And Go Jig

Butcher's March Jig

Butter Milk Mary's Jig

Buttermilk And Prattees Jig

Castle Garden Jig

Cat In The Hopper Jig

Catch Club Jig

Close To The Floor Jig

Come To The Raffle Jig

Come Under My Dimity

Connaught Man's Ramble Jig

Cowboy's Jig

Drink Of Brandy Jig

Drunken Gauger's Jig

Dublin Boy's Jig

Dusty Bob's Jig

Dusty Miller's Jig

Emon Acnuck Jig

Farewell, Sweet Nora Jig

Fasten The Wig On Her Jig

Flaming O'Flanigan's Jig

Fox Hunter's Jig

Frogs' Frolic Jig

The Gobby O' Jig

Golliber's Frolic Jig

Hare In The Corn Jig

Harrington's Hall Jig

Haste To The Wedding Jig

Hills Of Glenurchie Jig

Hop Jig

Humors Of Castle Lion Jig

Humour Of Glen Jig

Hunt The Fox Jig

Irish American Jig

Jackson's Rolling Jig

Johnny Hand's Jig

The Joy's Of Wedlock Jig

Katy Is Waiting Jig

Lady Cawdor's Jig

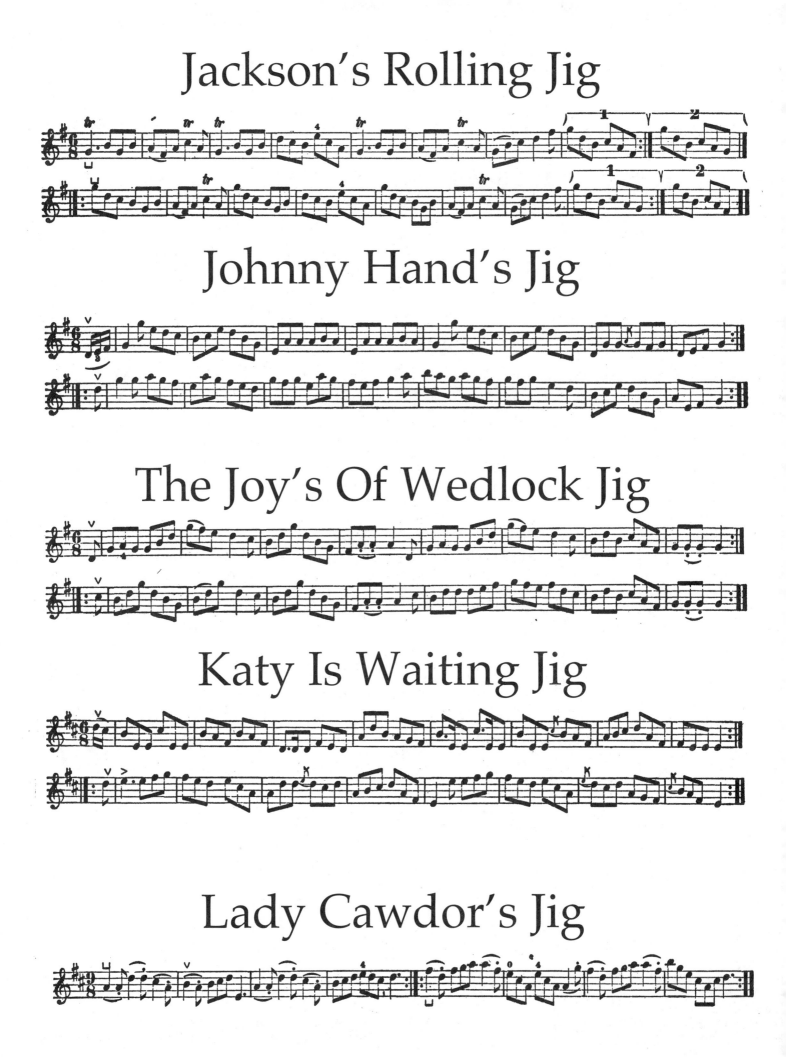

Lafrican's Jig

Lanigan's Ball Jig

Light And Airy Jig

Little Brown Jug Jig

The Limerick Lass Jig

Love Link's Jig

The Maid's Complaint Jig

Maloney's Fancy Jig

The Market Girl's Jig

Moll Roe In The Morning Jig

Moll Roe's Jig

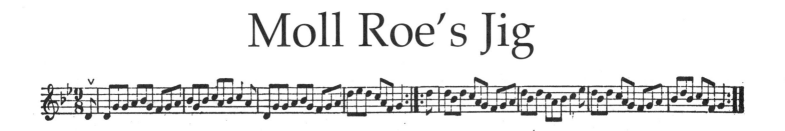

Mount Your Baggage Jig

Mrs. Hogan's Goose Jig

The Munster Lass Jig

My Pretty, Fair Maid Jig

D.C.

Mysteries Of Knock Jig

Neapolitan Threshers' Jig

The Night Of The Fun Jig

Night Of The Fair Jig

Old Figary O' Jig

Old Mother Goose Jig

Old Walls Of Liscarroll Jig

Over Land And Sea Jig

Owny's Best Jig

The Oyster Girl's Jig

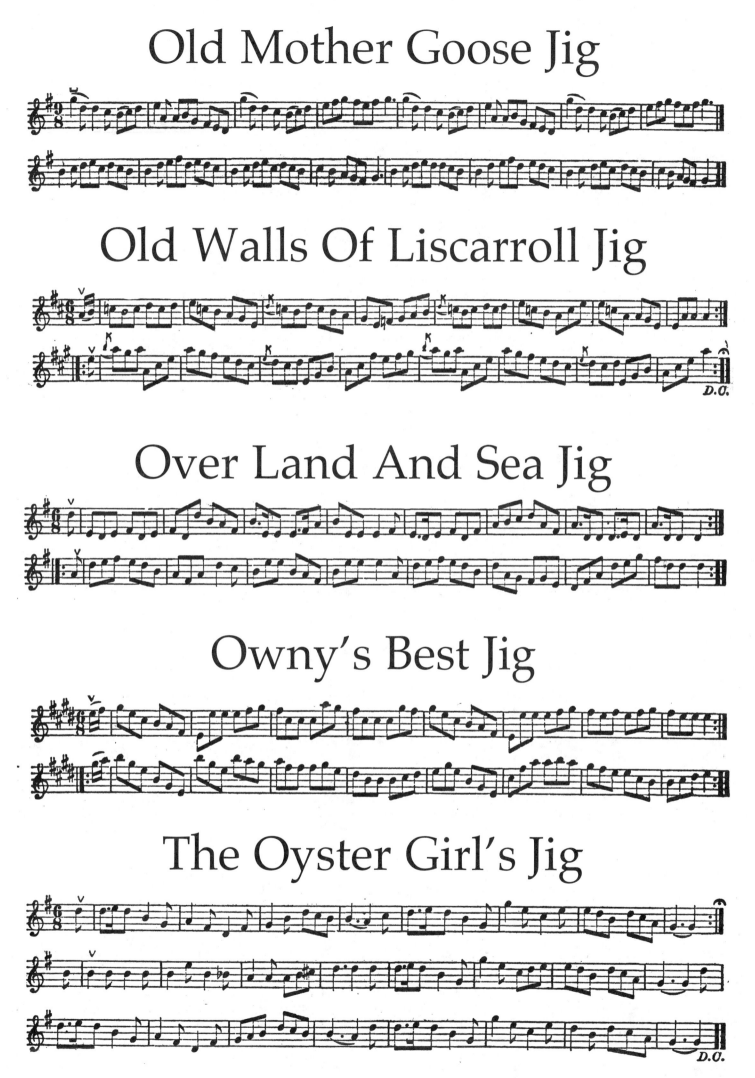

Paddy O'Carrol's Jig

Paddy's The Boy Jig

Paddy's Farewell To America Jig

Pandeen O'Rafferty Jig

Parnell And Ireland Jig

Pat In His Glory Jig

The Pausteen Fawn Jig

The Pivot Brig Jig

Prince Charles' Jig

Puss In The Corner Jig

The Rakes Of Westmeath' Jig

Ride A Mile Jig

Roaring Willies' Jig

Rocky Road To Dublin Jig

Rough Diamond Jig

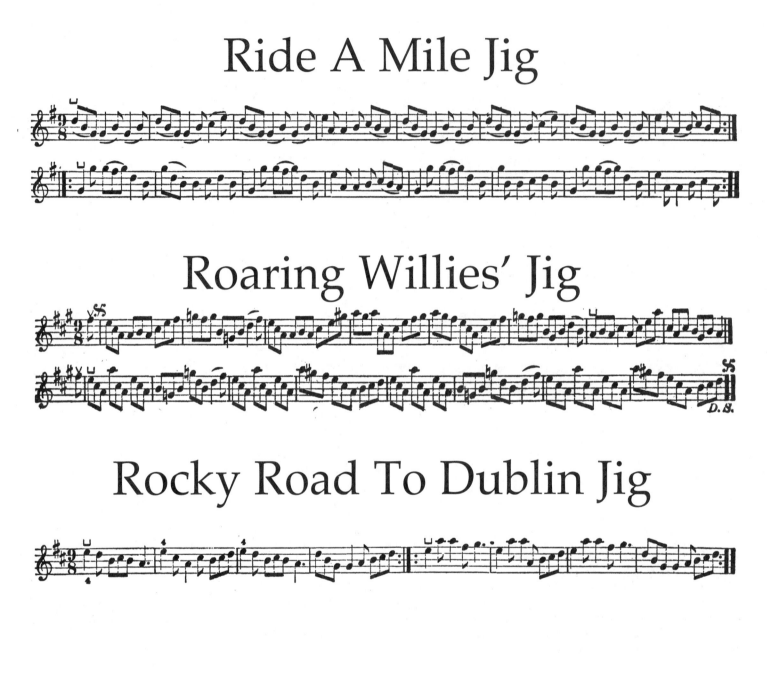

Sam Hide's Jig

Skin The Pealer Jig

The Soldier's Cloak Jig

Spirits Of Whiskey Jig

Strop The Razor Jig

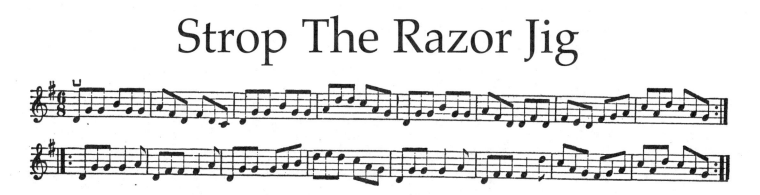

Sunday Is My Wedding Day Jig

To Cashell I'm Going Jig

Trip To Galway Jig

Two Penny Postman's Jig

Vaughan's Favorite Jig

1911

Street Fiddler - 1921

The Blind Fiddler

hornpipes

The word comes from a very old musical instrument called pipcorn in Wales, stockhorn in Scotland, and hornpipe in England. It was a double-reed instrument looking like a primeval oboe. Hornpipes date back as fas as 1260, and in the 18th century the Hornpipe dance was associated with sea-faring men, because dancing aboard ship was a form of exercise in those days and fiddlers were often a part of ship's company. The early time signature was 3/2 but in the last hundred years it has changed to common time. Hornpipes are generally played at a metronome setting of 180-♩

Acrobat's Hornpipe	Excelsior Hornpipe	Old Tanglefoot Hornpipe
Albemarle Hornpipe	Ferry Bridge Hornpipe	Palermo Hornpipe
Aldridge's Hornpipe	Fijiyama Hornpipe	Palmetto Hornpipe
Amateur Hornpipe	Flockton's Hornpipe	Parry's Hornpipe
Amazon Hornpipe	The Forester's Hornpipe	Passaic Hornpipe
Ariel Hornpipe	Globe Hornpipe	Peach-Blossom Hornpipe
Aspinwall Hornpipe	Globe Trotter Hornpipe	Poppy Leaf Hornpipe
Autograph Hornpipe	Golden Eagle Hornpipe	Portsmouth Hornpipe
Balkan Hornpipe	Here And There Hornpipe	Prince Albert's Hornpipe
Ball And Pin Hornpipe	Hiawatha Hornpipe	Princess Hornpipe
Beebe's Hornpipe	Highland Hornpipe	Randall's Hornpipe
Bee's Wings Hornpipe	Idyl Hornpipe	Red Lion Hornpipe
Belvidere Hornpipe	Jaunting Car Hornpipe	Rialto Hornpipe
Birmingham Hornpipe	Jim Clark's Hornpipe	Salem Hornpipe
Blanchard's Hornpipe	Jimmy Linn's Hornpipe	Sans Souci Hornpipe
Bonanza Hornpipe	Jinrikisha Hornpipe	Scotch Hornpipe
Brookside Hornpipe	Key West Hornpipe	Sebastopal Hornpipe
Celebrated Stop Hornpipe	Lamp-Lighters Hornpipe	Sentinal Hornpipe
Centennial Hornpipe	Lincoln's Hornpipe	Smith's Hornpipe
Champion Hornpipe	Locker's Hornpipe	Spirit Of 1881 Hornpipe
Coquette Hornpipe	London Hornpipe	Staten Island Hornpipe
Cosmopolitan Hornpipe	Lord Moira's Hornpipe	St. Botolph Hornpipe
Croton Hornpipe	Marshallhill's Hornpipe	St. Elmo Hornpipe
Cupido Hornpipe	Massasoit Hornpipe	Sumner's Hornpipe
Defiance Hornpipe	Minneapolis Hornpipe	Texarkana Hornpipe
De Golyer Hornpipe	Morning Fair Hornpipe	Thunder Hornpipe
Derby Hornpipe	National Guard's Hornpipe	Trafalgar Hornpipe
Dew Drop Hornpipe	Ned Kendall's Hornpipe	Union Hornpipe
Electric Hornpipe	New Century Hornpipe	Victoria Hornpipe
Eureka Hornpipe	Norfolk Hornpipe	Whiddon's Hornpipe
Every-Body's Hornpipe	North Star Hornpipe	
	Nymrod Hornpipe	

Acrobat's Hornpipe

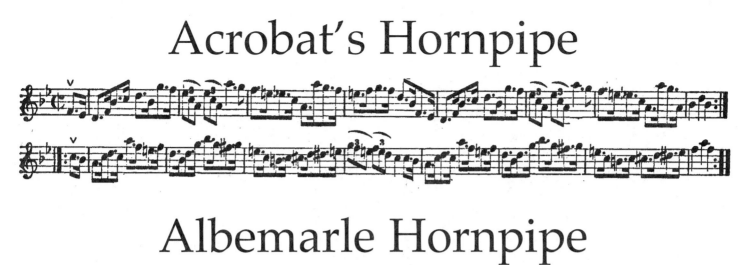

Albemarle Hornpipe

Aldridge's Hornpipe

Amateur Hornpipe

Amazon Hornpipe

Ariel Hornpipe

Aspinwall Hornpipe

Autograph Hornpipe

Balkan Hornpipe

Ball And Pin Hornpipe

Beebe's Hornpipe

Bee's Wings Hornpipe

Belvidere Hornpipe

Birmingham Hornpipe

Blanchard's Hornpipe

Bonanza Hornpipe

Brookside Hornpipe

Celebrated Stop Hornpipe

Centennial Hornpipe

Champion Hornpipe

Coquette Hornpipe

Cosmopolitan Hornpipe

Croton Hornpipe

Cupido Hornpipe

Defiance Hornpipe

De Golyer Hornpipe

Derby Hornpipe

Dew Drop Hornpipe

Electric Hornpipe

Eureka Hornpipe

Every-Body's Hornpipe

Excelsior Hornpipe

Ferry Bridge Hornpipe

Fijiyama Hornpipe

Flockton's Hornpipe

The Forester's Hornpipe

Globe Hornpipe

Globe Trotter Hornpipe

Golden Eagle Hornpipe

Here And There Hornpipe

Hiawatha Hornpipe

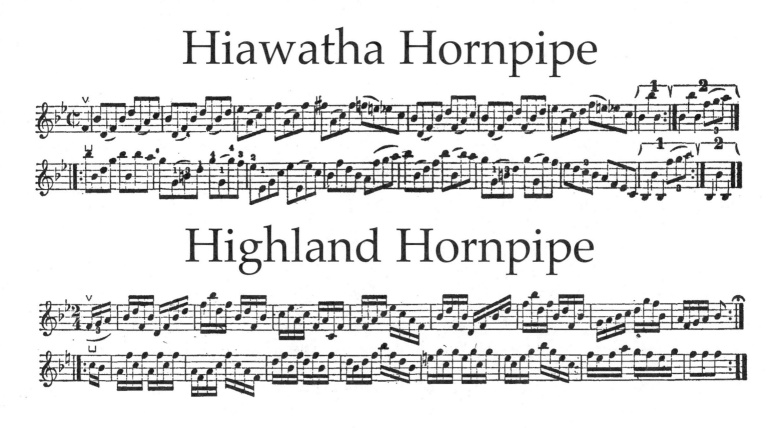

Highland Hornpipe

Idyl Hornpipe

Jaunting Car Hornpipe

Jim Clark's Hornpipe

Jimmy Linn's Hornpipe

Jinrikisha Hornpipe

Key West Hornpipe

Lamp-Lighters Hornpipe

Lincoln's Hornpipe

Locker's Hornpipe

London Hornpipe

Lord Moira's Hornpipe

Marshallhill's Hornpipe

Massasoit Hornpipe

Minneapolis Hornpipe

Morning Fair Hornpipe

National Guard's Hornpipe

Ned Kendall's Hornpipe

New Century Hornpipe

Norfolk Hornpipe

North Star Hornpipe

Nymrod Hornpipe

Old Tanglefoot Hornpipe

Palermo Hornpipe

Palmetto Hornpipe

Parry's Hornpipe

Passaic Hornpipe

Peach-Blossom Hornpipe

Poppy Leaf Hornpipe

Portsmouth Hornpipe

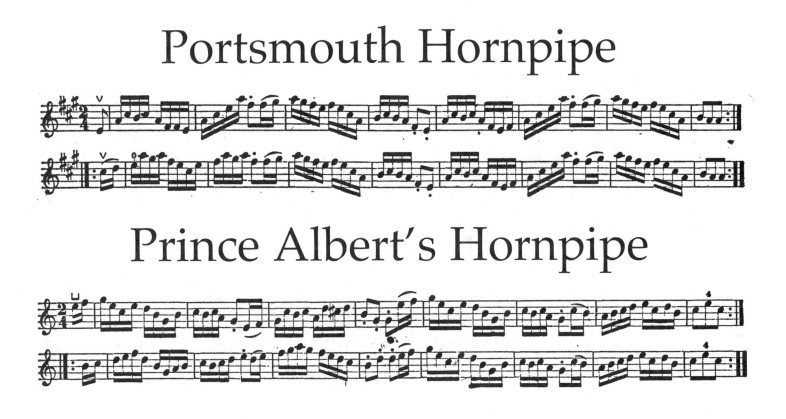

Prince Albert's Hornpipe

Princess Hornpipe

Randall's Hornpipe

Red Lion Hornpipe

Rialto Hornpipe

Salem Hornpipe

Sans Souci Hornpipe

Scotch Hornpipe

Sebastopal Hornpipe

Sentinal Hornpipe

Smith's Hornpipe

Spirit Of 1881 Hornpipe

Staten Island Hornpipe

St. Botolph Hornpipe

St. Elmo Hornpipe

Sumner's Hornpipe

Texarkana Hornpipe

Thunder Hornpipe

Trafalgar Hornpipe

Union Hornpipe

Victoria Hornpipe

Whiddon's Hornpipe

"Can you play The Monarch Clog?"   "Don't know it, I'll play Victoria Hornpipe." Monarch Clog?"

The Sheep Herder with Cowboy Laye's Band

Oscar Sholes and Booth Campell at the old Settlers Picnic,
Blanchard Springs, Arkansas, 1941

Highland Dancing

Highland Dancing

It is startling to first learn that in Scotland, Highland Dancing was once (and to an extent still is) and athletic event. But Scottish dances such as the Highland Fling and the Ghillie Callum (the Sword Dance) are in fact the solo dances of the Highland men, and are so vigorous that one must be in top physical shape to perform them. Long hours of practice are required for a dancer to become proficient enough to dance the intricate figures lightly and gracefully as they should be danced. Highland Dancing is far more enjoyable for the uninitiated and uninformed spectator if something is known of the history of the dance, the fine points to watch for, and how the dancers are judged on their performance. The following are some of the dances you might see in a competition.

THE HIGHLAND FLING

A dance of victory in battle. Traditionally, the ancient warriors and clansmen performed this dance on the small round shield (called a targ) which they carried into battle. One can understand the quick footwork and dexterity of the dancer when it is pointed out that most targs carried a pinpoint sharp spike of steel projecting some five or six inches from its center. A false or careless step could be more than a little painful.

THE SWORD DANCE

The ancient dance of war of the Scottish Gael. It is said to date back to King Malcolm Canmore. (See Gillie Calum.)

THE SEANN TRIUBHAS

Pronounced 'shawn trews' in the Gaelic language, it's translated into English as "old trousers." The dance has obscure origins. The movements and motions definitely depict a person in the act of shedding his breeks (britches) and the tradition is that of a Highlander who is impatient to get rid of the unfamiliar garment and get back to the freedom of his native Highland kilt.

THE IRISH JIG

A dance which may seem somewhat out of place at Scottish Games, but the dance is not peculiar to Ireland alone. It is equally popular and traditional in Scotland. However the Irish Jig danced at Highland Games is meant to be a parody of an Irishman/woman in an agitated state of mind. While the steps are traditional, the arm movements are not. Arm movements are an intrinsic part of Scottish dancing, and so the Scots added them to the Irish Jig in a humorous salute to their Celtic brethren across the Irish Sea.

THE SAILOR'S HORNPIPE

It was originally an ancient dance common to many parts of the British Isles. Its name derives from the instrument "horn pipe," comparable to the present day tin flute, which accompanied the dance. In time, the dance became so popular among sea-faring men that it became known as the "sailor's hornpipe." The modern dance is performed in nautical costume and imitates many typical shipboard activities usual in the days of wooden ships and iron men. You will readily spot rope hauling, climbing the shroud lines, and others.

THE SCOTTISH LLLT & FLORA MACDONALD

These are two of the dances known as the Scottish National dances. The attire worn by the females is different than for the Fling, Sword, etc. It is known as the Aboyne Dress, originating from the Aboyne Highland Games in Scotland where, up to this day, the wearing of the kilt is strictly forbidden for women. These dances are gentler, more flowing and are more graceful in nature than the other Highland dances. They still require a lot of skill to execute correctly. The music rhythms are different, too.

THE GILLIE CALUM

There is no Highland Dance older or better known than the Gillie Calum, or the Sword Dance. The tradition is that this Gillie Callum was no less than a personage than Calum-a-Chinn Mor (Malcolm Canmore) a Celtic Prince, who was a hero of a mortal combat against one of MacBeth's chiefs at the battle near Dunsinane in 1054, when he took his opponent's sword and crossed it with his own on the ground, symbolizing the sign of the Cross, and danced over them in exultation.

In support of this story the following quotation from "Carruther's History of Scotland" will afford further proof of this warrior's prowess in later years - "An incident happened which set both the courage and moderation of Malcolm in the fairest light. A group of villains had conspired to assassinate him, but the King, having discovered the plot went hunting near the place where they had laid their ambush, and calling the chief conspirator led him into a lonely valley surrounded with woods, where, unsheathing his sword, he thus addressed the traitor, "You seek my life - take it - setting aside ambushes, let valour decide who is the best fellow. " The culprit instantly threw himself at the monarch's feet and begged, and obtained, forgiveness (A.D. 1061)."

In 1057, Malcolm defeated and slew MacBeth at Lumphanan, Aberdeenshire, thus reacquiring all his father's kingdom: as recorded by Mariannus Scotus, the Scottish Monk of Cologne, and Tighernac, the Irish Analyst (both contemporaries), and also later by historians.

Set Dances And Miscellaneous

Set Dances are simply tunes to which different specific dances have been set.

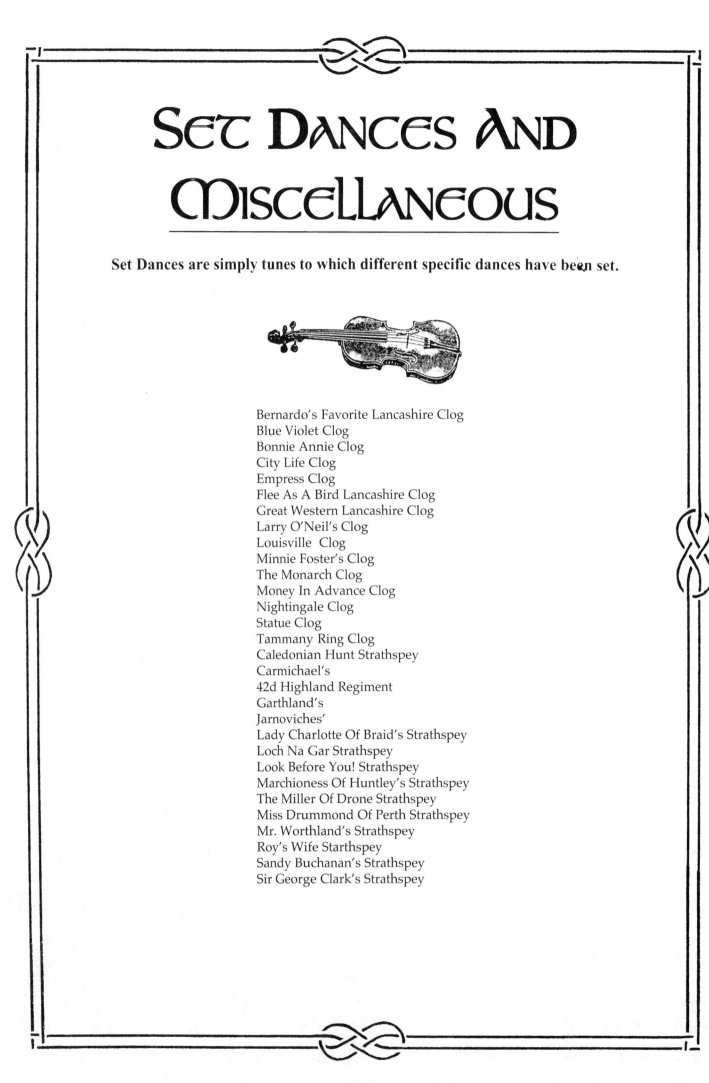

Bernardo's Favorite Lancashire Clog
Blue Violet Clog
Bonnie Annie Clog
City Life Clog
Empress Clog
Flee As A Bird Lancashire Clog
Great Western Lancashire Clog
Larry O'Neil's Clog
Louisville Clog
Minnie Foster's Clog
The Monarch Clog
Money In Advance Clog
Nightingale Clog
Statue Clog
Tammany Ring Clog
Caledonian Hunt Strathspey
Carmichael's
42d Highland Regiment
Garthland's
Jarnoviches'
Lady Charlotte Of Braid's Strathspey
Loch Na Gar Strathspey
Look Before You! Strathspey
Marchioness Of Huntley's Strathspey
The Miller Of Drone Strathspey
Miss Drummond Of Perth Strathspey
Mr. Worthland's Strathspey
Roy's Wife Starthspey
Sandy Buchanan's Strathspey
Sir George Clark's Strathspey

Bernardo's Favorite Lancashire Clog

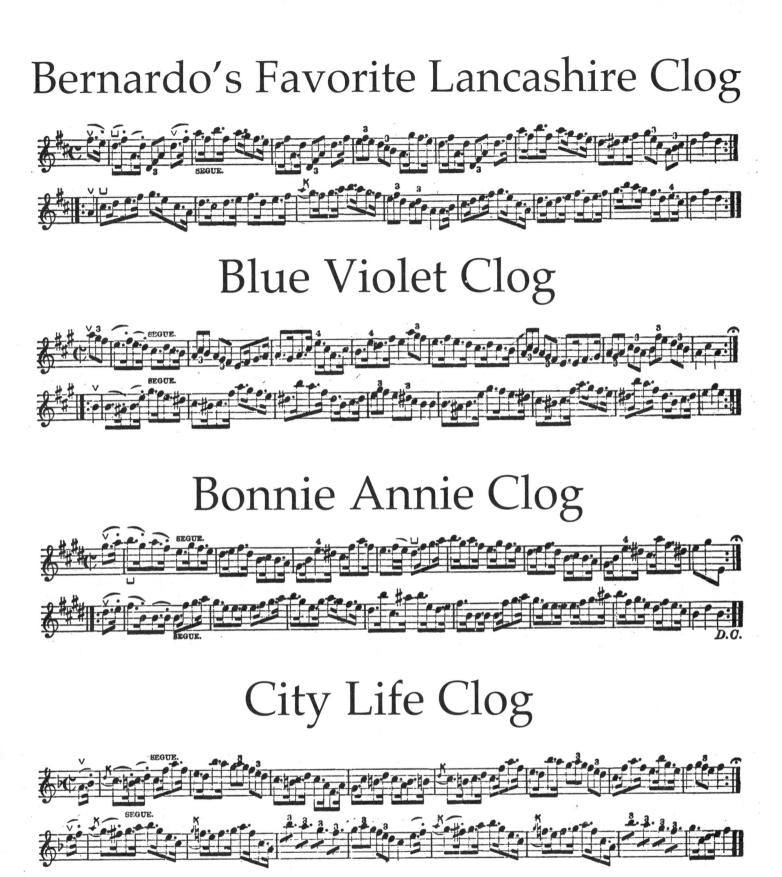

Blue Violet Clog

Bonnie Annie Clog

City Life Clog

Empress Clog

Flee As A Bird Lancashire Clog

Great Western Lancashire Clog

Larry O'Neil's Clog

Louisville Clog

Minnie Foster's Clog

The Monarch Clog

Money In Advance Clog

Nightingale Clog

Statue Clog

Tammany Ring Clog

Caledonian Hunt Strathspey

Carmichael's

42d Highland Regiment

Garthland's

Jarnoviches'

Lady Charlotte Of Braid's Strathspey

Loch Na Gar Strathspey

Look Before You! Strathspey

Marchioness Of Huntley's Strathspey

The Miller Of Drone Strathspey

Miss Drummond Of Perth Strathspey

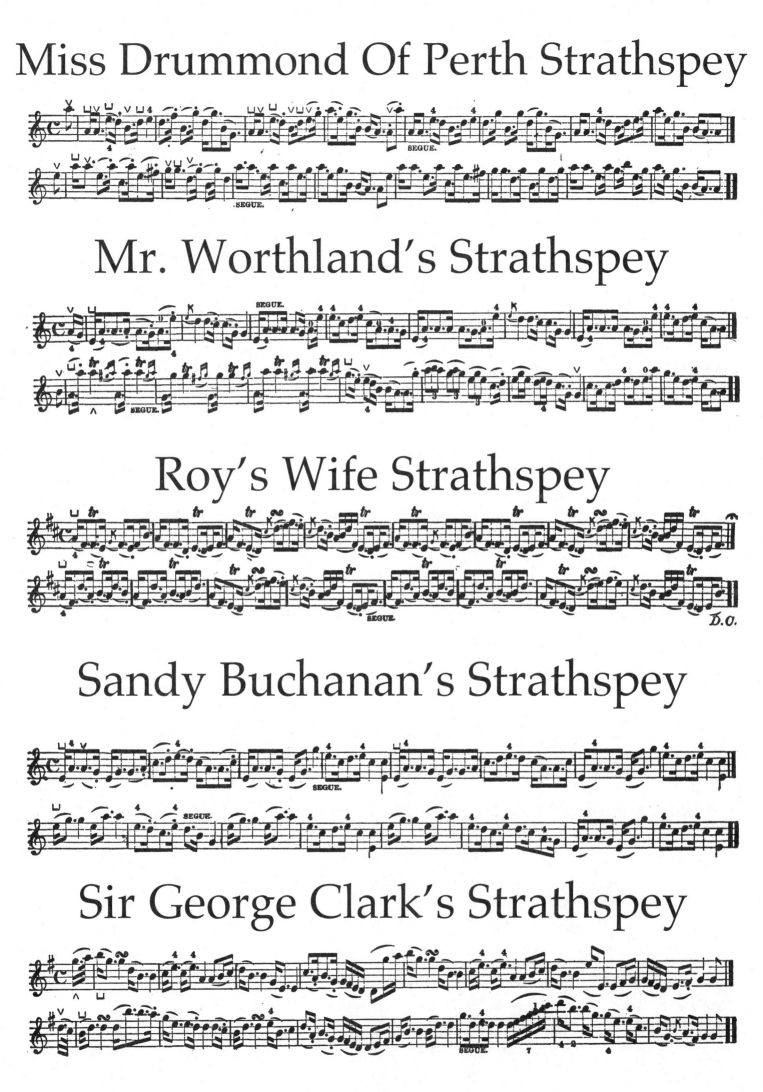

Mr. Worthland's Strathspey

Roy's Wife Strathspey

Sandy Buchanan's Strathspey

Sir George Clark's Strathspey